PICTURE WINDOW BOOKS
World Atlases

ATLAS of
North America

by Karen Foster

PICTURE WINDOW BOOKS
Minneapolis, Minnesota

First American edition published in 2008 by
Picture Window Books
5115 Excelsior Boulevard
Suite 232
Minneapolis, MN 55416
877-845-8392
www.picturewindowbooks.com

Editor: Jill Kalz
Designer: Hilary Wacholz
Page Production: Melissa Kes
Art Director: Nathan Gassman
Associate Managing Editor: Christianne Jones
Content Adviser: Lisa Thornquist, Ph.D., Geography
Cartographer: XNR Productions, Inc. (13, 15, 17, 19)

Editor and Compiler: Karen Foster
Factual Researcher: Joe Josephs
Designers: Fanny Masters & Maia Terry
Picture Researcher: Diana Morris
Illustrators: Rebecca Elliott and Q2 Media
Maps: Geo-Innovations UK

Printed in the United States of America.

Foster, Karen.
Atlas of North America / by Karen Foster. – Minneapolis, MN : Picture Window Books, 2008.
32 p. : col. ill., col. maps ; cm. – (Picture Window Books world atlases)
2-4
2-4.
Includes index and glossary.
ISBN 978-1-4048-3885-7
1. Maps – Juvenile literature. 2. North America – Geography – Juvenile literature.
3. North America – Maps for children.
E40.5   917 REF
2007004798   DLC

Photo Credits:
Roger Asbury/Shutterstock: 24t; Walter S. Becker/Shutterstock: 13b; Richard C. Bennett/Shutterstock: 21t; Larry Brandt/Shutterstock:
22br; Jason Cheever/Shutterstock: 11t; Matthew Collingwood/Shutterstock: 26t; Barbara Harvey/Shutterstock: 23t; Jan Butchofsky-
Houser/Corbis: 6c; George H.H. Huey/Corbis: 8b, 11b; Layne Kennedy/Corbis: 21b; Grigory Kubatyan/Shutterstock: 18bl; Kurt/Dreamstime:
compass rose on 4, 7, 9, 11, 13, 15, 17, 19, 25, 27; Danny Lehmann/Corbis: 18br, 21c; Charles & Josette Lenars/Corbis: 19bl; Stephanie Maze/
Corbis: 20t; Kelley-Mooney Photography/Corbis: 10b; Kevin R. Morris/Corbis: 24b; NASA/Corbis: 10t; Eric Nguyen/Jim Reed Photography/
Corbis: 12b; Kevin Norris/Shutterstock: 20b; Jesus Parazo/Shutterstock: 19br; PCL/Alamy: 27b; Marco Regalia/Shutterstock: 8t; Bill Ross/
Corbis: 9t; Bob Sacha/Corbis: 6b; Ariel Skelley/Corbis: 20c; Caroline K. Smith/Shutterstock: 23br; Paul A. Souders/Corbis: 23bl; Dale
C. Spartas/Corbis: 12t; Bill Stormont/Corbis; 8c; Christophe Testi/Shutterstock: 26b; Razman Toma/Shutterstock: 22tr; Graham Tomlin;
Shannon West/Shutterstock: 18t; Nik Wheeler/Corbis: 28-29; Stephan Widstrand/Corbis: 23tr

Editor's Note: The maps in this book were created with the Miller projection.

Table of Contents

Welcome to North America

The world is made up of five oceans and seven chunks of land called continents: North America, South America, Antarctica, Europe, Africa, Asia, and Australia. This map shows North America's position in the world.

Arctic Circle

NORTH AMERICA

Atlantic Ocean

Tropic of Cancer

Pacific Ocean

Equator

SOUTH AMERICA

Tropic of Capricorn

Legend
A legend tells you the title of a map and what the map's symbols mean.

SOUTH AMERICA	Continent
Pacific Ocean	Ocean

Antarctic Circle

The Antarctic Circle is an imaginary line in the southern part of the world that marks the edge of the Antarctic region.

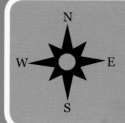

Compass Rose
A compass rose shows you the four cardinal directions: north (N), south (S), east (E), and west (W).

North America is the world's third-largest continent. It is made up of three large countries—Canada, the United States of America, and Mexico—as well as Greenland, the seven countries in Central America, and the many Caribbean islands.

North Pole

Arctic Ocean

The Arctic Circle is an imaginary line in the northern part of the world that marks the edge of the Arctic region.

Arctic Circle

EUROPE

ASIA

The Tropic of Cancer and the Tropic of Capricorn are imaginary lines north and south of the equator. Places that lie between the two lines are hot and wet.

Tropic of Cancer

Pacific Ocean

AFRICA

Indian Ocean

Equator

The equator is an imaginary line around the middle of the world.

AUSTRALIA

Tropic of Capricorn

Southern Ocean

Antarctic Circle

ANTARCTICA

South Pole

Scale Bar
A scale bar helps measure distance. It tells you the difference between distances on a map and the actual distances on Earth's surface.

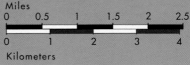

Miles
0   0.5   1   1.5   2   2.5

0   1   2   3   4
Kilometers

5

Countries

The continent of North America is made up of six main regions: Greenland, Canada, the United States, Mexico, Central America, and the Caribbean islands. There are 23 countries in North America.

Canada is the continent's largest country. It is also the second-largest country in the world (after Russia). The smallest country is Saint Kitts and Nevis.

Some islands are their own countries, with their own governments. But some islands are governed by other countries. Greenland, for example, belongs to Denmark. Puerto Rico belongs to the United States.

What's on the menu?

Barbados – stewed conch with sweet potatoes

Belize – mangoes, papayas, and other fruits

Canada – cheese curds, fries, and gravy

Costa Rica – spicy beans and rice

Cuba – meat patty with potato sticks

Grenada – codfish, chili, and coconut milk stew

Guatemala – corn tortillas

Jamaica – fried ackee (a fruit) and codfish

Mexico – corn husk-wrapped bean tamales

Nicaragua – tres leches (three milks) cake

United States – cheeseburger and fries

Mexican mariachi bands play trumpets, guitars, and violins. The musicians wear fancy jackets and wide hats.

Jazz music was invented by African-Americans 100 years ago.

Speaking to each other

Most North Americans speak English or Spanish. French is spoken in parts of Canada and in Haiti. The people of Greenland speak Danish and Greenlandic.

ANTIGUA AND
BARBUDA

THE BAHAMAS

BARBADOS

BELIZE

CANADA

COSTA RICA

CUBA

DOMINICA

DOMINICAN
REPUBLIC

Arctic Ocean

GREENLAND
(DENMARK)

Arctic Circle

CANADA

Pacific Ocean

UNITED STATES

Atlantic Ocean

Miles
0   300   600   900 1,200 1,500

0   600   1,200   1,800   2,400
Kilometers

THE BAHAMAS

Tropic of Cancer

MEXICO

CUBA

HAITI

PUERTO RICO (U.S.A.)

JAMAICA

ANTIGUA &
BARBUDA

DOMINICAN
REPUBLIC

DOMINICA

ST. KITTS
& NEVIS

BARBADOS

BELIZE

GUATEMALA   HONDURAS

EL SALVADOR   NICARAGUA

ST. LUCIA

GRENADA

COSTA RICA   PANAMA

ST. VINCENT &
THE GRENADINES

TRINIDAD
& TOBAGO

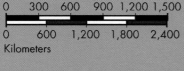
EL SALVADOR

N
W   E
S

GRENADA

GUATEMALA

HAITI

HONDURAS

JAMAICA

MEXICO

NICARAGUA

PANAMA

SAINT KITTS
AND NEVIS

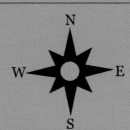
SAINT LUCIA

SAINT VINCENT
AND THE
GRENADINES

TRINIDAD AND
TOBAGO

UNITED
STATES

7

Landforms

The land of North America takes many shapes—from mountains to deep canyons to low-lying plains.

The peaks of the Rocky Mountains, or Rockies, stretch through the western region of North America about 2,000 miles (3,200 kilometers) into Mexico. In Mexico, the mountains are called the Sierra Madre Oriental and the Sierra Madre Occidental.

Parts of North America stick out into the ocean as peninsulas, while other parts are completely surrounded by water.

A smoking mountain

A volcano is a kind of mountain that can throw hot, melted rock (lava), ashes, and gases from inside Earth. Mexico has many volcanoes. Popocatépetl is one of the active ones. Although it smokes, the mountaintop is covered with snow all year long.

The name Popocatépetl *means "smoking mountain."*

Mesas

Flat-topped towers of layered rock called mesas are found in the deserts and canyons of the southwestern United States.

The word mesa *means "table" in Spanish.*

Grand Canyon

North America's Grand Canyon is the largest canyon in the world. Its deep valley was carved out by the Colorado River. The steep sides of the canyon are made from layers of rock. Some of the rocks are about 2 billion years old.

At sunset, the rock walls of the Grand Canyon seem to change color.

- Mount McKinley is not only the highest mountain in the United States, it's also the highest mountain in North America.
- Greenland is the largest island in the world.
- Canada has the world's longest coastline.

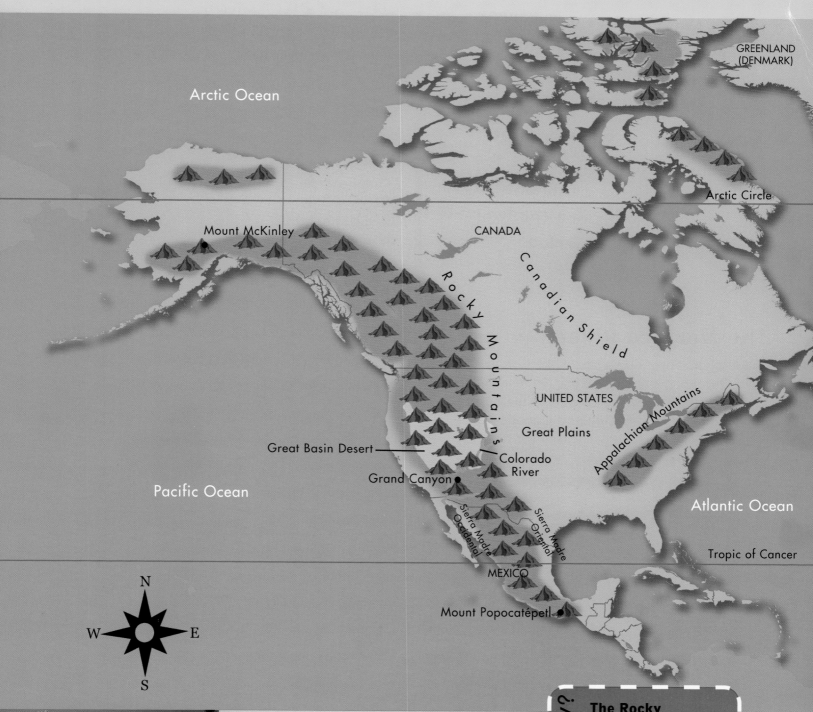

Arctic Ocean

GREENLAND (DENMARK)

Arctic Circle

Mount McKinley

CANADA

Canadian Shield

Rocky Mountains

UNITED STATES

Great Plains

Appalachian Mountains

Great Basin Desert

Colorado River

Grand Canyon

Pacific Ocean

Atlantic Ocean

Sierra Madre Occidental

Sierra Madre Oriental

Tropic of Cancer

MEXICO

Mount Popocatépetl

N
W E
S

Dozens of national parks lie along
the Rocky Mountains in Canada,
the United States, and Mexico.

*The towering Rocky Mountains are covered
with snow most of the year.*

DID YOU KNOW? The Rocky
Mountains are the
"backbone" of
the continent. The
slopes are dotted
with lakes and
covered with thick
evergreen forests.

9

Bodies of Water

North America has many large rivers and lakes. Canada has more lakes and inland water than any other country in the world.

The Mississippi River and the Missouri River flow across the lower half of the continent. These two major rivers are the longest rivers in North America.

The Niagara River

The Niagara River flows from Lake Erie to Lake Ontario, a distance of just 35 miles (56 kilometers). It serves as part of the border between the United States and Canada. At the river's midway point, water spills over a steep cliff, forming Niagara Falls.

A tour boat sails past the spray of Niagara Falls.

The Great Lakes

The Great Lakes are the largest group of freshwater lakes on Earth. They form part of the border between Canada and the United States. The five Great Lakes, from west to east, are Superior, Michigan, Huron, Erie, and Ontario. Lake Superior is the largest freshwater lake in the world.

Lake Michigan (bottom left) looks like a long, blue finger when viewed from space.

Lake Nicaragua

Lake Nicaragua is the largest freshwater lake in Central America. It is about 100 miles (160 km) long and up to 45 miles (72 km) wide. Once part of the Caribbean Sea, the lake is home to many saltwater fish that have adapted to their new surroundings.

- Salt Lake City, United States, is built on the dried-out bed of a huge salt lake.

- The Rio Grande forms a natural border between part of Mexico and the United States. The river supplies water to the surrounding land, making it easier for people to grow crops in the dry soil.

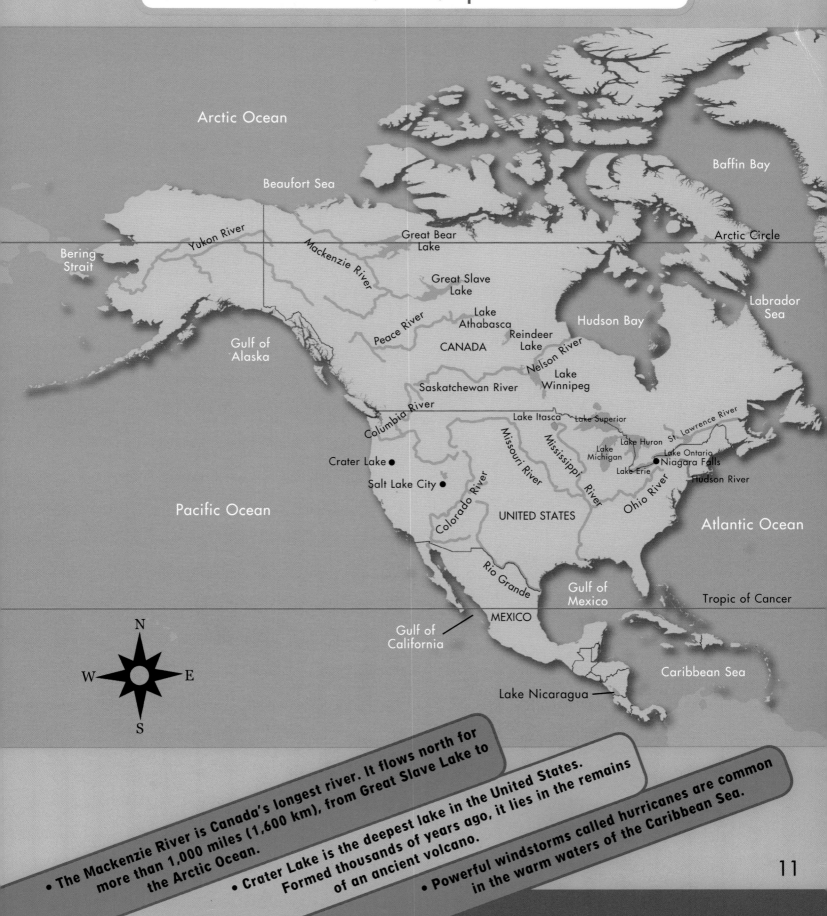

Arctic Ocean

Baffin Bay

Beaufort Sea

Yukon River

Mackenzie River

Great Bear Lake

Arctic Circle

Bering Strait

Great Slave Lake

Labrador Sea

Peace River

Lake Athabasca

Hudson Bay

Gulf of Alaska

CANADA

Reindeer Lake

Nelson River

Saskatchewan River

Lake Winnipeg

Columbia River

Lake Itasca

Lake Superior

St. Lawrence River

Lake Huron

Lake Michigan

Lake Ontario

Crater Lake ●

Missouri River

Mississippi River

● Niagara Falls

Salt Lake City ●

Lake Erie

Hudson River

Pacific Ocean

Colorado River

UNITED STATES

Ohio River

Atlantic Ocean

Rio Grande

Gulf of Mexico

Tropic of Cancer

N
W   E
S

Gulf of California

MEXICO

Caribbean Sea

Lake Nicaragua

- The Mackenzie River is Canada's longest river. It flows north for more than 1,000 miles (1,600 km), from Great Slave Lake to the Arctic Ocean.

- Crater Lake is the deepest lake in the United States. Formed thousands of years ago, it lies in the remains of an ancient volcano.

- Powerful windstorms called hurricanes are common in the warm waters of the Caribbean Sea.

Climate

Climate is the average weather a place has from season to season, year to year. Rainfall and temperature play large parts in a region's climate.

Because North America stretches from above the Arctic Circle to below the Tropic of Cancer, it has a wide range of climates.

The United States is so large that it has six different kinds of climate. Its northern-most places have a cold polar climate, while its southern-most places have a hot tropical climate.

Continental climate

Much of Canada and one-fourth of the United States has a continental climate. This region has four separate seasons: a cool spring and fall, a warm to hot summer, and a cold winter. In fall, when the weather gets colder, the leaves of trees such as maple and birch turn red and gold and drop to the ground.

Maple trees are the most colorful in fall.

Hot and cold

The continent of North America has some of the hottest and coldest temperatures on Earth. In July 1913, Death Valley, United States, recorded the second-hottest temperature in the world. It was 134 degrees Fahrenheit (57 degrees Celsius). In February 1947, Snag, in far northwestern Canada, recorded the third-coldest temperature on Earth. It was minus 81 F (minus 63 C).

Climate basics

A region's climate depends upon three major things: how close it is to the ocean, how high up it is, and how close it is to the equator. Areas along the ocean have milder climates than areas farther inland. The higher a region is, and the farther it is from the equator, the colder its temperature.

- Panama is North America's southern-most country. Because it lies close to the equator, temperatures average a warm 80 F (27 C) year-round.

- Most of Central America has a tropical climate. Some areas receive more than 240 inches (610 centimeters) of rain each year.

- The islands in the Caribbean Sea have hot, wet summers and warm, fairly dry winters. The islands' wettest months are May through October.

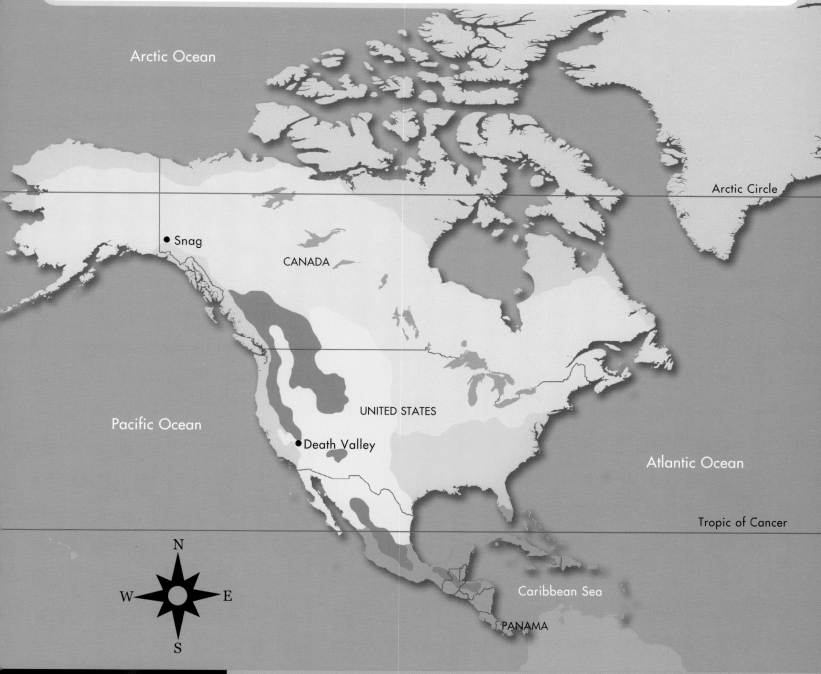

Climate

dry	dry most or all year with hot summers and warm to cold winters
polar	dry and cold all year
mountain	wet and dry seasons, cool to cold all year
mild	wet winters or all year with warm to hot summers and cool winters
tropical	wet and dry seasons, hot all year
continental	wet, warm to hot summers and cold winters

—— country boundary

Arctic Ocean

Arctic Circle

• Snag

CANADA

Pacific Ocean

UNITED STATES

• Death Valley

Atlantic Ocean

N
W   E
S

Tropic of Cancer

Caribbean Sea

PANAMA

In the far northern parts of North America, the Arctic winter is long, dark, and cold. At night, the sky often lights up with shimmering colors known as the northern lights.

The northern lights glow in many different colors.

Plants

Because of its many ecosystems, North America is home to a wide variety of plants. An ecosystem is all of the living and nonliving things in a certain area. It includes plants, animals, soil, weather ... everything!

Plants such as cactuses have adapted to the hot, dry conditions of North America's desert ecosystems by storing water. Prairie grasses have deep roots so they can survive wildfires. Forests of evergreens, maples, and other hardy trees can be found across one-third of the continent.

Some Plants of North America

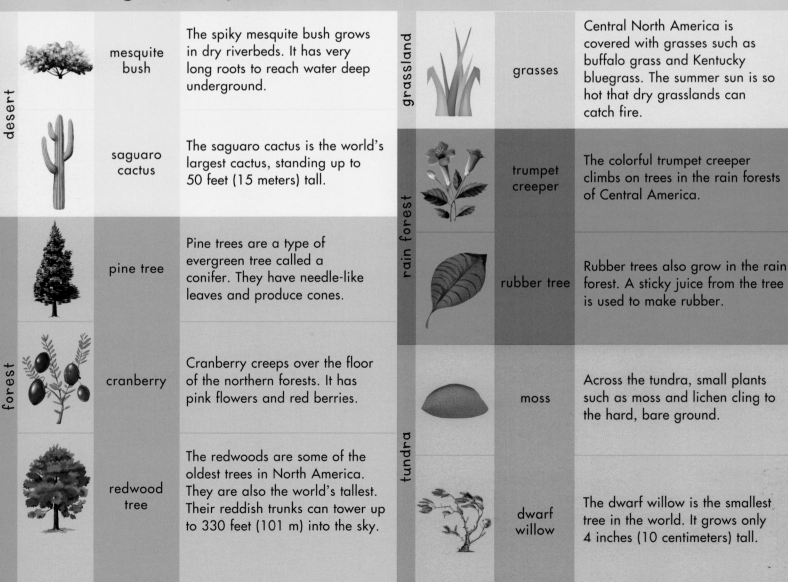

desert

mesquite bush	The spiky mesquite bush grows in dry riverbeds. It has very long roots to reach water deep underground.
saguaro cactus	The saguaro cactus is the world's largest cactus, standing up to 50 feet (15 meters) tall.

forest

pine tree	Pine trees are a type of evergreen tree called a conifer. They have needle-like leaves and produce cones.
cranberry	Cranberry creeps over the floor of the northern forests. It has pink flowers and red berries.
redwood tree	The redwoods are some of the oldest trees in North America. They are also the world's tallest. Their reddish trunks can tower up to 330 feet (101 m) into the sky.

grassland

grasses	Central North America is covered with grasses such as buffalo grass and Kentucky bluegrass. The summer sun is so hot that dry grasslands can catch fire.

rain forest

trumpet creeper	The colorful trumpet creeper climbs on trees in the rain forests of Central America.
rubber tree	Rubber trees also grow in the rain forest. A sticky juice from the tree is used to make rubber.

tundra

moss	Across the tundra, small plants such as moss and lichen cling to the hard, bare ground.
dwarf willow	The dwarf willow is the smallest tree in the world. It grows only 4 inches (10 centimeters) tall.

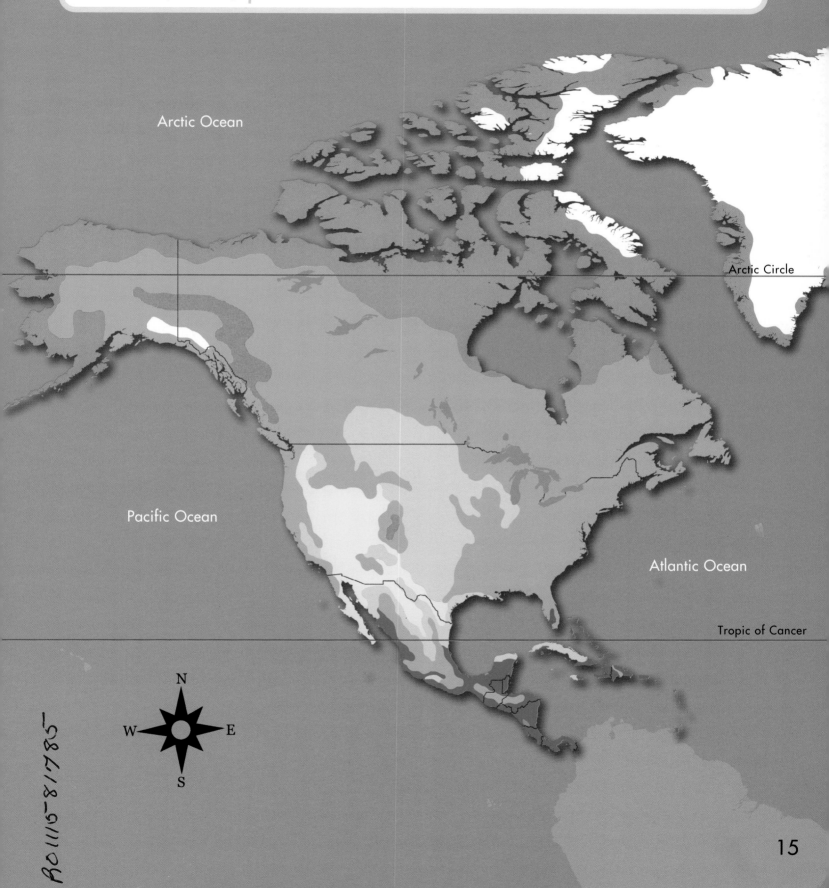

Major Ecosystems

—— country boundary

desert	grassland	mountain	tundra
forest	ice cap	rain forest	wetlands

Arctic Ocean

Arctic Circle

Pacific Ocean

Atlantic Ocean

Tropic of Cancer

N
W   E
S

15

Animals

Many different types of animals live in North America, and they are all well-adapted to the ecosystems in which they live. An ecosystem is all of the living and nonliving things in a certain area.

Moose, bears, and other animals that live in North America's tundra ecosystems have thick fur to keep them warm through the long winters. In the desert, animals such as coyotes have light-colored fur that reflects the hot sunlight and keeps them cool.

Some Animals of North America

ecosystem	animal	description
desert	coyote	Coyotes hunt for small animals, such as jackrabbits and mice.
desert	goose	In the spring, geese fly north to nesting grounds in Canada. In the fall, they fly south to spend the winter in sunny Mexico.
forest	beaver	The beaver cuts down trees with its strong teeth and builds dams in streams and rivers.
forest	puma	Pumas are large wild cats that can live in a variety of ecosystems, including forests, mountains, and grasslands.
forest	bald eagle	The bald eagle can be found across Canada and the United States. It lives near water where there are fish to eat. It also needs tall trees to nest in.
grassland	prairie dog	Prairie dogs are small, furry squirrel-like animals that live in burrows underground.
grassland	monarch butterfly	Each year, hundreds of monarch butterflies fly from summer homes in Canada to winter in Mexico.
rain forest	toucan	The toucan is a fruit-eating bird with a huge, yellow bill. It lives high in the rain forest trees.
tundra	grizzly bear	Grizzlies are very large brown bears. They eat fruit, honey, berries, and small animals.
tundra	moose	The moose is a large deer with humped shoulders and huge antlers. It lives in the snowy forests and swamps of the North.
wetlands	American alligator	American alligators are found in rivers, swamps, ponds, and other watery areas of the southeastern United States.

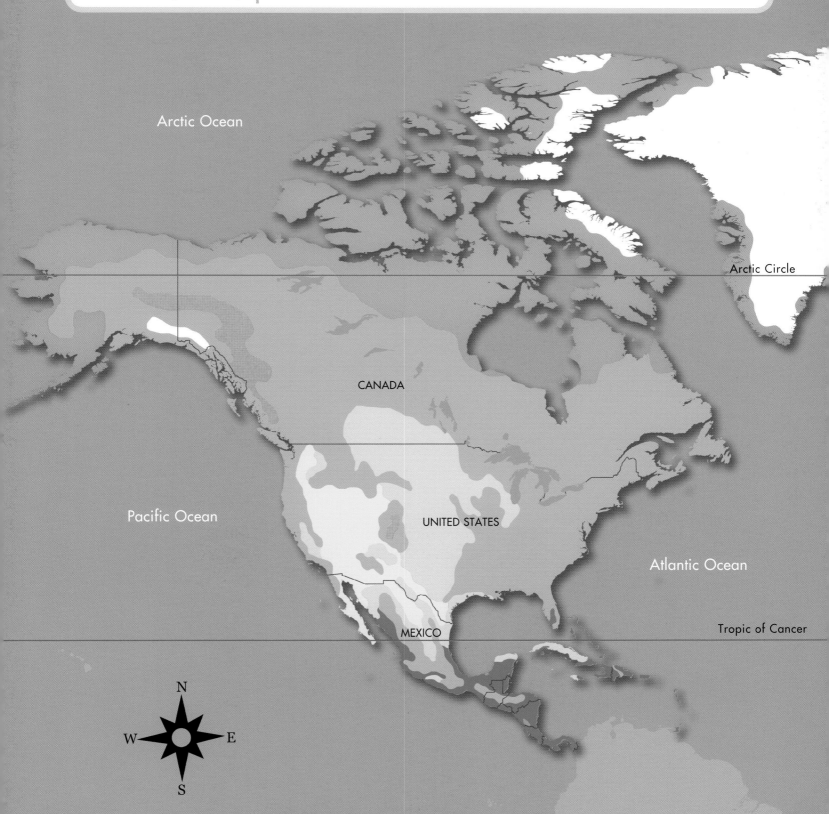

Major Ecosystems

—— country boundary

| desert | grassland | mountain | tundra |
| forest | ice cap | rain forest | wetlands |

Arctic Ocean

Arctic Circle

CANADA

Pacific Ocean

UNITED STATES

Atlantic Ocean

MEXICO

Tropic of Cancer

N
W E
S

Population

More than two-thirds of North America's population live in cities. Mexico City is the most populated city on the continent.

Most North Americans live near bodies of water. The water can be used for power, for jobs, and for fun. It can also be used to grow crops and to transport goods and people.

There are large areas in North America where very few people live. For example, few people want to live in northern Canada, where the winters are long, cold, and dark.

Half of Guatemala's population lives in Guatemala City, the country's capital and the largest city in Central America.

Four important cities

San Francisco, United States, is home to about 750,000 people. One of the city's most famous areas is Chinatown. Many Chinese families live there.

A typical building in Chinatown, San Francisco

Santo Domingo, Dominican Republic, is the second-largest city in the Caribbean (Havana, Cuba, is the largest). Located on the country's southern coast, the city of about 4 million people is a major port.

Montréal is a busy Canadian port city. Located on the banks of the St. Lawrence River, Montréal is a center for industry, business, and culture. Nearly 3.5 million people live there.

One of the biggest cities in the world, **Mexico City**, Mexico, is home to about 20 million people. It was built on the site of an ancient Aztec city called Tenochtitlan.

The lights of Mexico City

- Aside from the West Coast, few people live in the western half of the United States. The land is used mostly for farming, ranching, and recreation.
- In most Central American and Caribbean countries, about half of the population lives in the countries' capital cities.

People per Square Mile

- ● place of interest
- —— country boundary

less than 5	5-25	25-125	125-250	more than 250
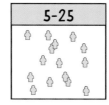	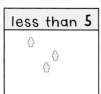	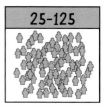	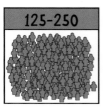	

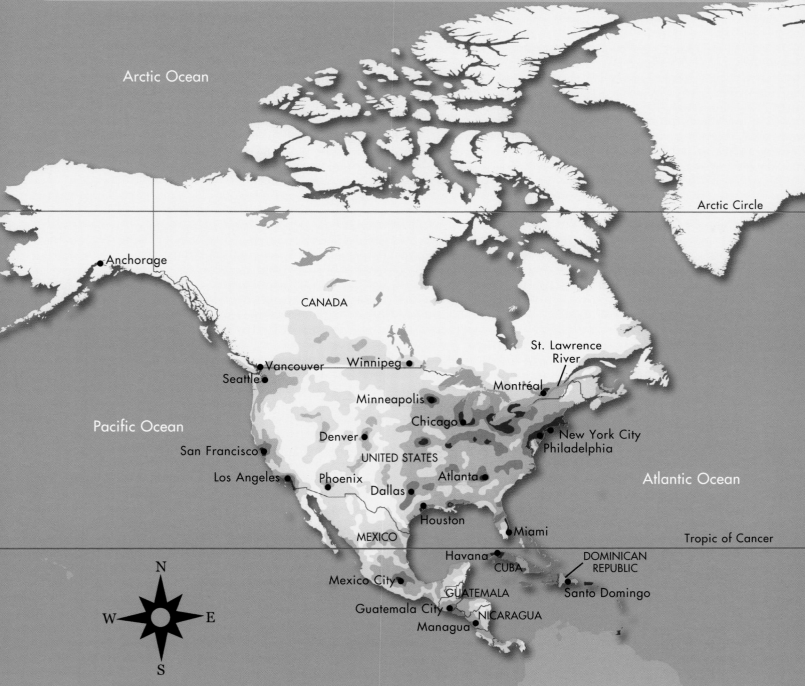

Arctic Ocean

Arctic Circle

Anchorage

CANADA

Pacific Ocean

Vancouver
Seattle
Winnipeg

St. Lawrence River

Minneapolis
Montréal

Chicago

Denver
New York City
Philadelphia

San Francisco

UNITED STATES

Los Angeles
Phoenix
Atlanta

Atlantic Ocean

Dallas

Houston

Miami

MEXICO

Tropic of Cancer

Havana
DOMINICAN REPUBLIC

CUBA

Mexico City
Santo Domingo

GUATEMALA

Guatemala City
NICARAGUA

Managua

N
W E
S

Besides the Inuit, very few people live in northern North America.

The Inuit live in villages near and inside the cold Arctic Circle.

More than half of the U.S. population lives in large cities along the coasts.

Southern U.S. coastlines are often lined with buildings.

19

People and Customs

The people of North America are a mixture of many different cultures from around the world. Together with the Native Americans, they make the continent an exciting place to live.

Spanish culture

Mexico, Central America, and many of the Caribbean islands were once ruled by Spain. Because of this fact, most people in these regions speak Spanish. They also practice Roman Catholicism, the religion most Spaniards practice. Spanish touches can be seen in the regions' art, food, music, and more.

In Mexico, outdoor markets of flowers, fruits and vegetables, and crafts are much like those in Spain.

Independence Day

On July 4, 1776, the American Colonies declared their freedom from Britain. Since then, July 4 has been known in the United States as Independence Day. Each year, people celebrate with parades, picnics, and fireworks.

U.S. children march in an Independence Day parade.

Sports

Millions of people in North America enjoy watching and playing baseball and basketball. Soccer is very popular in Mexico and Central America. Hockey is a favorite sport in Canada.

Hockey players battle it out on the ice.

American Indians

American Indians have lived in North America for thousands and thousands of years. Today, many of them live on special lands called reservations.

An American Indian performs a traditional dance.

Folk art

The Purepecha and the Huichol tribes of Mexico still speak their native Indian language and keep ancient customs. The Purepecha make folk art from wood and clay, handpainting it in bright colors. The Huichol are known for their yarn paintings and beadwork.

Purepecha dolls are brightly colored.

The Inuit

The largest group of people living in the Far North of North America are the Inuit. In the past, the Inuit people survived by hunting and trapping. Today, many of them work in the mining, building, and tourism industries. Some still travel by dogsled. Others use snowmobiles.

A team of dogs pulls a sled over the ice.

Postcard Places

Here are some of North America's special places of interest.

Head-Smashed-In Buffalo Jump

Canada

American Indians used to hunt bison at Canada's Head-Smashed-In Buffalo Jump by chasing them over a cliff.

Chichen Itza

Mexico

Long ago, the Mayan people built cities in the jungles of Mexico and Central America. The crumbling ruins of their pyramids at Chichen Itza still survive today.

GREENLAND

Mount McKinley

Head-Smashed-In Buffalo Jump

Yellowstone National Park

Mount Rushmore

Chichen Itza

JAMAICA

Caribbean Cool

Tourists flock to Caribbean island countries such as Jamaica to enjoy the sandy beaches.

Herds of bison roam wild in the United States' Yellowstone National Park. The park has many natural wonders.

Meet the Presidents

Mount Rushmore

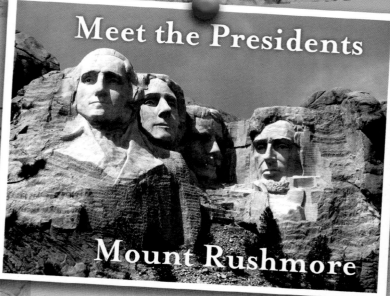

Mount Rushmore is a set of huge carved-rock faces of former U.S. presidents George Washington, Thomas Jefferson, Theodore Roosevelt, and Abraham Lincoln.

Yellowstone National Park

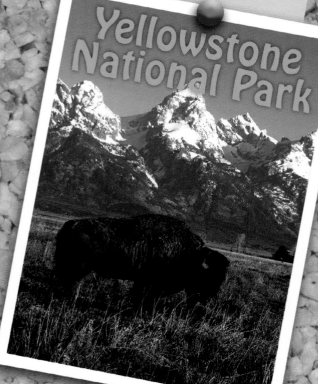

Mount McKinley is the highest mountain on the continent of North America.

On top of the world

Mount McKinley

Greetings from Greenland

Most of Greenland lies above the Arctic Circle. It is a land of giant icebergs and mountains of snow.

23

Growing and Making

North America has many natural resources. Forests that supply timber (wood used for furniture and houses) cover a large part of the land.

Farmland throughout the continent produces corn, cotton, soybeans, wheat, and other crops. North America grows more food than any other continent in the world.

The continent also has large amounts of coal, copper, iron ore, oil, natural gas, and silver.

Oil and natural gas

Oil and natural gas provide northwestern North America with most of its wealth. The Trans-Alaska Pipeline carries oil from the drilling sites to ports along the coast.

Huge pipes carry oil across northern North America.

Timber forests cover about 25 percent of Canada's land. Cut logs are sometimes moved from place to place by floating them downriver.

Mexico's fruit exports

Mexico is the seventh-largest exporter of fresh fruit in the world. Nearly 90 percent of those exports go to the United States. Mexico's major fruit exports include avocados, grapes, lemons, strawberries, and limes.

- Coffee is an important export for most countries in Central America and for many countries in the Caribbean, including the Dominican Republic, Cuba, and Haiti.
- Beneath the seafloor off the eastern coast of Mexico lie large amounts of oil and natural gas.

Major Natural Resources, Land Use, and Industry

● place of interest
— country boundary

Technology
Manufacturing
Ranching
Forestry
Tourism
Natural Gas
Oil
Fishing
Mining
Farming: cotton · wheat · fruit · coffee

Arctic Ocean

Trans-Alaska Pipeline

Arctic Circle

CANADA

Pacific Ocean

UNITED STATES

Atlantic Ocean

MEXICO

THE BAHAMAS   Tropic of Cancer

CUBA

DOMINICAN REPUBLIC

HAITI

N
W   E
S

- The leading industry in many Caribbean islands is tourism. In the Bahamas, for example, more than 60 percent of the country's wealth comes from tourism.

- The United States is the second-largest cotton producer in the world. China is the largest.

- The heart of North America is often called the world's "breadbasket" because so much grain is grown there.

Transportation

People and goods are moved across North America in three major ways: by water (rivers, canals), by land (highways, railways), and by air (airplane routes).

Bordered by three oceans, North America has many large port cities. Ships transport goods to and from places all over the world.

St. Lawrence Seaway

The St. Lawrence River is an important transportation route in the East. Parts of the river have been turned into canals. The canals form a seaway that links the five Great Lakes with the Atlantic Ocean.

Large ships carry goods from North America's Great Lakes to the Atlantic Ocean.

Crossing the bridge

The Golden Gate bridge, in the U.S. city of San Francisco, is a very important transportation link. It connects San Francisco with places to the north. About 40 million vehicles cross the Golden Gate bridge every year.

The Golden Gate bridge stretches nearly 2 miles (3.2 kilometers).

The Canadian Pacific Railway

Built more than 100 years ago, the Canadian Pacific Railway, or CPR, was Canada's first cross-country railroad. Today, the CPR runs from Montréal to the Pacific coast.

Panama Canal

The man-made Panama Canal links the Atlantic and Pacific Oceans. Ships save thousands of miles and many days by using the canal instead of sailing around the tip of South America. About 12,000 ships pass through the Panama Canal every year. It is one of the world's busiest waterways.

Major Transportation Routes

● place of interest ——— country boundary

——— major highway   ——— major waterway   ——— major railroad

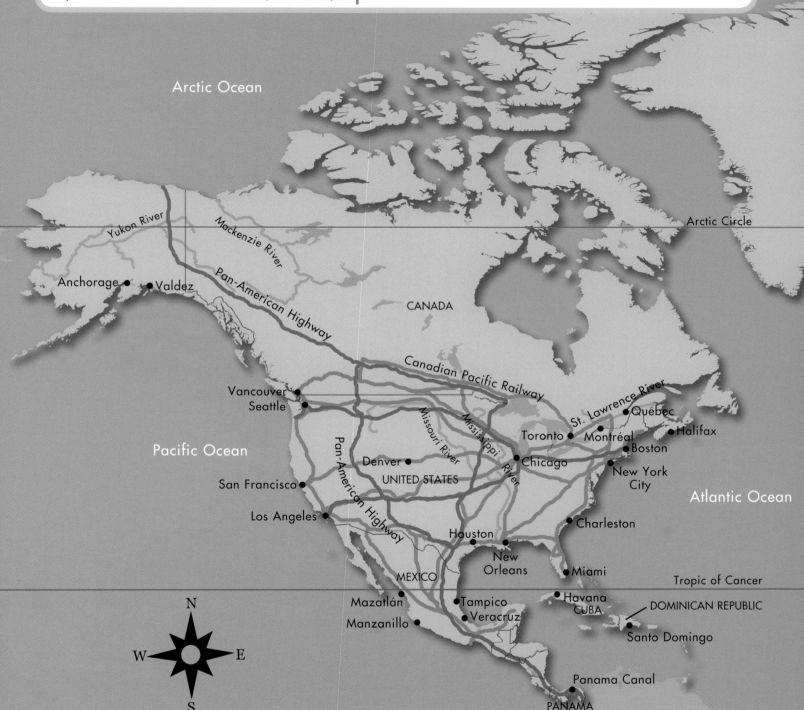

Arctic Ocean

Yukon River

Mackenzie River

Pan-American Highway

Arctic Circle

Anchorage ● ● Valdez

CANADA

Canadian Pacific Railway

St. Lawrence River

Vancouver ●
Seattle ●

● Québec
● Montréal
● Halifax

Toronto ●

● Boston

Pacific Ocean

Missouri River

Mississippi River

Chicago ●

Denver ●

● New York City

San Francisco ●

UNITED STATES

Pan-American Highway

Atlantic Ocean

Los Angeles ●

● Charleston

Houston ●

New Orleans ●

MEXICO

● Miami

Tropic of Cancer

N
W E
S

Mazatlán ●

Tampico ●
Veracruz ●

Havana ● CUBA

DOMINICAN REPUBLIC

Manzanillo ●

Santo Domingo ●

Panama Canal ●

PANAMA

Pan-American Highway

The Pan-American Highway is a huge network of roads. It stretches from northwestern North America to the lower regions of South America.

The Pan-American Highway runs through 15 countries.

27

Journey Up the Mississippi

The luggage is loaded. Everyone is onboard. The paddle-wheeler is ready to leave!

Puffs of steam shoot from the smokestacks. The passengers crowded on deck are excited. This is the start of their trip up the Mississippi River, the longest river in North America. The journey begins in the city of New Orleans, United States, and will end upriver, in Minneapolis.

Soon, New Orleans, the home of jazz music, is left behind. The boat glides past stretches of farmland, where cotton, rice, and other crops are grown.

Memphis lies just ahead. Another famous music city, Memphis is known as the birthplace of the blues. It is also famous for its pork barbecue.

Farther upriver, the passengers see wildlife. On the bank, beavers collect wood to build their homes. Bald eagles fly overhead, swooping for fish. Brown pelicans dip their bills into the water to scoop out crayfish and eels.

The river widens, and the boat chugs past St. Louis. The mighty Missouri River joins the Mississippi River here. The boat captain slows down to steer around the sandbars.

Long, flat-bottomed boats called barges float by in the opposite direction. They carry oil, coal, steel, and logs downriver. The barges honk their horns in greeting. The paddle-wheeler answers with a loud whistle or two.

The land flattens out as the boat passes through large fields of wheat. There are still many miles to go. The boat will end its journey at Minneapolis. But the Mississippi River will continue farther north, narrowing until it reaches its source at Lake Itasca.

The Mississippi River

The Mississippi River is often used as a dividing line when talking about the western United States and the eastern United States. Because it is the largest, most important river in North America, the Mississippi has been given many nicknames through the years. Nicknames include Big River, Old Man River, and Ole Miss.

North America At-a-Glance

Continent size: the third-largest of Earth's seven continents

Number of countries: 23

Major languages:
- English
- French
- Spanish

Total population: 542 million (2005 estimate)

Largest country (land size): Canada

Most populated country: United States

Most populated city: Mexico City, Mexico

Climate: mostly mild and continental; polar in Greenland and northern Canada; dry in the West; tropical in the South; cool to cold in the mountains

Highest point: Mount McKinley, United States, 20,320 feet (6,198 meters)

Lowest point: Death Valley, United States, 282 feet (86 m) below sea level

Longest river: Mississippi River

Largest body of water: Lake Superior

Largest desert: Great Basin Desert

Major agricultural products:
- beans
- coffee
- corn
- cotton
- dairy products
- soybeans
- sugar/sugarcane
- tropical fruits
- wheat

Major industries:
- agriculture
- fishing
- forestry
- mining
- manufacturing (machinery, clothing, paper, electronics, chemicals, and motor vehicles)

Natural resources:
- coal
- copper
- gold
- iron ore
- natural gas
- nickel
- oil
- silver

Glossary

body of water – a mass of water that is in one area; such as a river, lake, or ocean

boundary – a line that shows the border of a country, state, or other land area

canyon – a deep valley with very steep sides

climate – the average weather a place has from season to season, year to year

compass rose – a symbol used to show direction on a map

continent – one of seven large land masses on Earth, including Africa, Antarctica, Asia, Australia, Europe, North America, and South America

crops – plants that are grown in large amounts and are used for food or income

desert – a hot or cold, very dry area that has few plants growing on it

ecosystem – all of the living and nonliving things in a certain area, including plants, animals, soil, and weather

equator – an imaginary line around Earth; it divides the northern and southern hemispheres

export – to send goods to another country to be sold or traded

forest – land covered by trees and plants

forestry – the work of growing and caring for forests

grassland – land covered mostly with grass

inland – away from the coast

island – land that is completely surrounded by water

lake – a body of water that is completely surrounded by land

landform – a natural feature on Earth's surface

legend – the part of a map that explains the meaning of the map's symbols

mountain – a mass of land that rises high above the land that surrounds it

natural resources – materials such as water, trees, and minerals that are found in nature

North Pole – the northern-most point on Earth

ocean – the large body of saltwater that covers most of Earth's surface

peninsula – a body of land that is surrounded by water on three sides

plain – an area of flat or nearly flat land

population – the total number of people who live in one area

port – a place where ships can load or unload cargo (goods or people)

rain forest – a thick forest that receives a lot of rain year-round

ranching – the work of raising animals such as cattle and sheep on a ranch

river – a large stream of water that empties into a lake, ocean, or other river

scale – the size of a map or model compared to the actual size of things they stand for

South Pole – the southern-most point on Earth

species – groups of animals or plants that have many things in common

temperature – how hot or cold something is

tundra – land with no trees that lies in the arctic regions

valley – a low place between mountains or hills

wetland – an area that has very wet soil and is covered with water at least part of the year

Index

On the Web

FactHound offers a safe, fun way to find Web sites related to topics in this book.
All of the sites on FactHound have been researched by our staff.

1. Visit www.facthound.com
2. Type in this special code: 1404838856
3. Click on the FETCH IT button.

Your trusty FactHound will fetch the best sites for you!

Look for all of the books in the Picture Window Books World Atlases series:

Atlas of Africa

Atlas of Australia

Atlas of Europe

Atlas of North America

Atlas of South America

Atlas of Southwest and Central Asia

Atlas of the Far East and Southeast Asia

Atlas of the Poles and Oceans